CONTENTS

Preface

This guidebook shares simple mindset changes that we used with my native Hawaiian husband who suffered a catastrophic, bi-thalamic stroke. Although he regained full control of his body, he lost vast amounts of memory and was subsequently diagnosed as cognitively impaired. Using the techniques offered in this book as well as many positive Hawaiian perspectives on health and healing, my husband became the man he was before the stroke. He steadily regained his memory and is living life with a renewed sense of confidence and energy.

In the pages that follow, each topic is offered in clear terms and is broken down into a brief, yet detailed discussion on how my family used these empowering techniques to help him reclaim his memories. At the end of this book in section 14, ways to empower caregivers, as well as those they care for, is shared. Life is not just about surviving, it is about retaining our deep connections to the past, recognizing the value of the present moment, and visualizing all the adventures we dream of sharing in the future.

Mana Psychology™

EMPOWERED TO REMEMBER

A Guide to Reclaiming Memories

Keti Kamalani
Michelle Shine, Ph.D.

Dedicated to my husband and everyone who stood
by him throughout his recovery.
We hope his journey will help empower yours.

1
Mana Psychology™
& Hawaiian Empowerment?

Ancient Hawaiians understood the importance of inner empowerment. They called this power *Mana*. Mana Psychology™ focuses on empowered mindfulness for improving and nurturing the mind from within. We offer a series of guidebooks to empower healthy mindfulness. Based on a single case study, this guide offers you simple, easy-to-use methods to reclaim lost memories and inspire the mind to remember.

Mana Psychology™ techniques to empower the mind were adapted from the first book in our original series entitled, *Mana Gardening, Empower Yourself & Live a Better Life.* These valuable skills are based on ancient Hawaiian transpersonal psychology and cognitive behavioral techniques that can help you feel energized, or relaxed, as wanted or needed, anytime, anywhere.

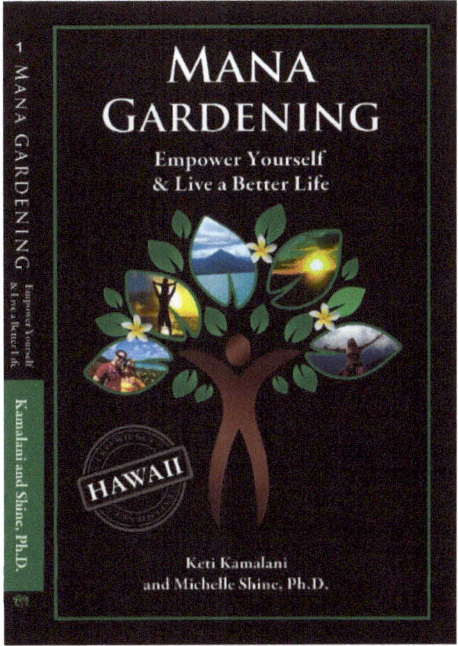

This Mana Psychology™ guidebook proposes simple mindset shifts that aided my husband in reclaiming lost memories. These methods not only led to a return of memories, but also an improved sense of confidence for him as well as all those who assisted in this journey. The methods are combined with Hawaiian healing concepts and Mana Gardening™ On-The-Go Meditation which offer patients and caregivers significant moments of stress relief throughout their busy day. Most appealing is the fact that these methods do not require additional work or additional therapy; they simply require approaching the problem of memory loss differently. To learn more ways you can help yourself and others retrain the brain, empower your mind, body and spirit, visit

www.managardening.com.

2
Living With Memory Loss

Memory loss is a devastating condition. Medical professionals use the term *cognitive impairment* to identify measurable memory loss. The word cognitive is defined as relating to, being, or involving conscious intellectual activity, such as thinking, reasoning, or remembering. Cognitive impairment can occur from trauma, medication side effects, metabolic and/or endocrine disorders, delirium, illness, depression, and dementia. Cognitive disorders lead to a high burden of suffering for patients, families, and society.

Assessment for cognitive impairment requires a complete medical exam by a primary care physician (PCP) to recognize, identify, and treat underlying medical conditions. If you or someone you love is struggling with memory loss, see a doctor first to ensure that you do not overlook a treatable medical problem.

A diagnosis of cognitive impairment can be complicated. Often it involves a conversation between the clinician, patient, and family members (or other persons who can provide insight to changes the patient may not recognize). Respectful communication is the foundation to navigating every aspect of health and healing for those with cognitive disorders as they may not be able to articulate their needs or fears.

Families struggling with a cognitively impaired loved one often feel completely overwhelmed. Having lived with and loved someone with memory loss, I am keenly aware that the majority of current medical support for those with memory loss is focused on dealing, and not on healing.

In spite of all the best intentions, support offered by PCPs and therapists consist of methods focused on solely coexisting with those suffering from memory loss. Medications to calm and control the emotions of the cognitively impaired are often prescribed to support the goal of coexisting with one another and can lead to further memory loss (see side effects). Options for healing or for regaining memory are not offered nor explored. This results in a life sentence of suffering for the cognitively impaired and their families.

With limited options, physicians, mental health professionals, social workers, and researchers must expand their ideas to new frontiers that involve healing. We can better serve those in need by focusing our energy on new behavioral interventions that improve the day-to-day life experience of those who are affected by cognitive disorders and those who care for them.

Empowered To Remember takes you through a series of simple cognitive behavioral Mana Psychology™ methods to aid in reclaiming memory. These simple mindset changes that were implemented within our family profoundly improved my husband's life and not only returned his memory, but also helped him to regain the ability to access and store old and new memories. In reclaiming his memories, he regained his life. Our family no longer feels burdened with caring for a cognitively impaired individual. I know this truly works because we lived it and I watched this method transform the man I love back to the man I have always loved. My hope in writing this, is that it will help others enduring such difficult circumstances.

3
Hawaiian Terms & Perspectives

Hawaiians believe that everything has a positive spiritual strength or **Mana**. The term **Mana loa** means great power and ancient Hawaiians recognized that personal empowerment is vital to health and healing. The unique aspect of caring for others in the Hawaiian culture is the need to empower not just the cared for, but also the caregiver. We must care for our own wellbeing and understand that in being empowered we are then called upon to safeguard the dignity, and *Mana* of those who are suffering.

When working with those who need healing we must come to them with an abundance of our own personal power so that we can help without taking and give without leaving ourselves needy. Caregivers must actively strive to be rested, well-fed, patient, calm, kind, and emotionally well-grounded. We are guardians of our *Mana* and the *Mana* of those we care for.

The word **Malama** means to care for, tend, and protect. The word **Pono** means completely, properly, carefully. The phrase **Malama e pono,** means to take good care, with forthright devotion. However, in the Hawaiian culture, this means to do right by yourself and others. Empowered in caring for others, you are called upon to tend to them with the same care you give to yourself.

Caregivers often give to the point they are exhausted and tend to forget their own needs. Christian cultures use the phrase, "Love thy neighbor as thy self," and often overlook the importance of "thy self". In caring for ourselves, we take our needs off the list of work for others. To help someone else heal, we must **Malama e pono** not only for their needs, but also our own.

Hawaiian wisdom believes that empowering the mind and spirit has positive effects on the body. Western medicine is beginning to acknowledge what ancient practices have believed for all time – that the body believes what the mind tells it. With cognitive injuries or illnesses, the repair process requires enormous energy and nourishment. *Mana* is a unique force as it is energy-giving and should be seen as powerful fuel for the regenerative healing that is needed to reclaim memories.

Ancient Hawaiians also practiced a deep exhale known for its healing powers. It is considered the breath of life and is called the **Ha**. Western cultures emphasize a deep inhale, forgetting that the ability to inhale deeply is driven by the depth of the exhale. In learning to exhale completely we become fully oxygenated, which is fundamental to healing. Reclaiming memories is like big wave surfing – it requires great strength, the right board and a big wave. Think of *Mana* as superior strength, the *Ha* as your best surfboard, and the mind as the perfect wave.

4
The Value of Mindfulness

Mindfulness is the psychological process of paying attention to the present. It is necessary to be aware of what is going on right here, right now. We must strive to actively be more thoughtful, recognize mindless distractions and try to be fully present. Sadly, with social media, cell phones, and video games we are learning to disappear from those we love. When my father, Papa Vic came to live with us in the final years of his life, our family had to become fully present. Recognizing the trip hazards of a toy left on the floor was easy, however understanding the lack of dignity one experiences when they are in need, took much more effort.

Whenever we asked Papa Vic if he wanted anything he always said, "No." He did not want to be a burden. With mindfulness we realized that through asking him, he unintentionally became self-rejected. We stopped asking and made a simple kitchen rule: if you make anything for yourself, make the same for Papa Vic. If he was sleeping, we sat it down with a note. If he was awake, we enjoyed the snack or beverage together. With a shift in awareness, we empowered him to be more engaged with us and we were all better people for it. There are many ways to become present with those you care for. Years later, we were able to give my husband the same mindfulness we had given my father, Papa Vic.

5
Our View of Synaptic Pruning

For many years the world view was that our brain was hardwired by age three. Challenging that view, scientists discovered that not much is actually known about the brain at all. There are many competing ideas for how the brain works, or how the brain can be medicated, but we have limited known options for healing the brain.

In a process called synaptic pruning, the brain naturally trims its cells and connections to improve its abilities and performance without the loss of memory. The brain acts much like a gardener cutting back weaker or less useful synapses to permit healthier neural activity. Let us think of synaptic connections in the brain as branches and the stored images and memories as leaves. With synaptic pruning, the brain trims off weaker branches, transferring the wealth of information in each leaf before trimming.

When you have an injury or a cognitive disorder, trimming still occurs but memories don't get transferred first. As the branches which are suddenly dead, or perhaps broken, get cut off, the memories on each branch become detached like fallen leaves and become disconnected from neural activity. The brain is busy reorganizing itself like a gardener cutting off dead branches and it does not go back for the information stored in the old leaves. Science holds to the belief that once these branches are cut, the memories stored in each leaf are lost. In our world of advanced medicine, the lost memories of these fallen leaves are accepted as fate and we do not look for ways to restore these memories.

In caring for my husband, no one spoke to me about how we could help him regain his memories. I was met with options on how to deal with his impairment and was only offered a dismal glimpse into a life of survival guided only with ways to cope. I was given many choices to fake being happy through medicating myself or him, through finding caregivers to help me with him, or using support counselors to help us deal with the tragedy of his memory loss. I wanted to heal him and could not accept a lifelong sentence of hopelessness.

Michelle and I were actively writing a series of books on what we call *Mana Gardening,* a method of using inner perspective changes to re-write and empower the way we navigated our everyday lives. In *Mana Gardening,* Michelle and I often built "new memories" to help us see the present and the past with less negativity and grief.

We adapted this same technique with my husband in an effort to help him heal and feel empowered too. It was a simple change in which we stopped pushing him to remember, and instead we remembered for him. We immediately saw profound changes in his desire to thrive rather than survive and soon discovered that whenever we shared our memories about past events, which we call *new "old" memories*, he organically recalled more and more of the details around that past experience.

When we shared our memory of a past event with my husband, it was as if the new "old" memory inspired the growth of a shiny new leaf on a budding branch that stimulated the brain to go back and look at the old fallen leaves. In our view, the brain is like a happy gardener that begins to rake up all the old leaves and sort them into piles to put them where they belong. It is not an instant process as the brain still has an entire garden to tend to and prune, but it seemed that once the new leaf appeared, the brain understood that there was now a place to put the details that matched the new "old" memory – much like the Memory game we played a child. When the brain recognized something it had seen before, it tried to make the match!

In part 9, we guide you through how we went about rebuilding these new "old" memories. For now, consider that the brain is far more capable of restoring lost memories than we are being taught to believe. This case study raises the awareness that we may actually be able to heal memory loss instead of just dealing with the cognitively impaired.

In our case study we also found that the brain is highly self-protective. It is no coincidence that the brain suppresses harmful memories and recalls happy ones. To get the brain engaged in sorting through this pile of old information, we discovered we had to reach for the leaves that held the sweetest memories. In working with my husband after his stroke, we have a new view of synaptic pruning – we now see that it is dynamic with far more possibilities than we ever imagined.

If we want the brain to work with us on pruning and relocating old stored memories to new locations, we have to start by working to retrieve memories that have the highest and healthiest emotional connections. We have to make synaptic pruning a fun and joyous reunion of the old with the new. We have to turn on the music that goes with the song and we have to dance to that music as we relive those happy memories. The brain loves a party! The brain loves love, it loves music, it loves laughter, it needs the sound of familiar, happy voices, and craves to be with everything we see as beautiful.

With new "old" memories, you are more or less building a starter leaf for your loved one, then their brain can find the matching leaves of memories that were cut off the branch. If you give them a positive image their brain will pick up the leaves that go with that image and give them back their memories!

We must surround the cognitively impaired with everything they feel joyously connected to and lay down the new "old" memories first. We cannot ask our loved one to remember their favorite flower or ask them if this is the flower they like. We must lead with the flower in hand, and we must proclaim that, "This is your favorite flower, and wow, it smells heavenly!"

6
Ho'oponopono is the First Step

The Hawaiian culture teaches the practice of **Ho'oponopono,** which means to make things right. In Hawaii this practice is commonly used when you have a falling out with another person. No matter whose fault it is, putting an effort in to making things right can release negativity and transform your life in a positive way.

Ho'opnopono, requires only four statements to be made. These are: I am sorry. Please forgive me. I love you. Thank you.

These statements can be said to forgive ourselves as well as others. When caring for a person who has a cognitive impairment, say these words as a daily ritual for yourself and for them. The impaired do not need to take part in it. You can say these words to a mirror. The power of this is amazing and it should be the first step to working with the impaired. You may need to make everything right between you and them every single day. It will allow you to release any negative feelings about yourself or your impaired loved one. It will give you peace. When caring for the impaired, *Ho'opnopono* is a way to let go of all guilt, anger and frustration that accompanies working with the cognitively impaired.

When repairing healthy committed relationships, *Ho'oponopono* can be done directly with the person that you disagree with. If the other person is someone you cannot trust, we suggest you read our original book, *Mana Gardening, Empower Yourself and Live & Better Life,* to discover how you can easily make things right from within. With our techniques, you do not have to work with anyone else, it only takes you.

7
Every Conversation is New

Working with someone suffering from memory loss can be exhausting and frightening. Caregivers are often life partners who are alone with all of the work it takes to care for themselves and their loved one. It is scary to think of all the "what if's." What if they get worse? What if I get sick? What if they forget me?

The fears are real, the responsibility of being the only person to remember everything is stressful and there is no relief in sight. The overwhelming work it takes to care for someone with memory loss places care givers at a high risk for personal health problems.

How can caregivers help the impaired reclaim memories without making life harder than it already is? The first steps involve very simple changes in perspective. We begin with a commitment to see every conversation as new. This mindset change rescues the caregiver from feeling trapped in a repetitive cycle and helps the patient remain engaged in making connections within their everyday life.

We stop saying things like, "You already told me that," or, "You keep forgetting." We start engaging in every conversation and stop mentioning their loss. We quit inadvertently stealing their *Mana* by verbally punishing them for forgetting. We start listening for and celebrating when new words or ideas are added to what we know as "the same old story". We become present to our time with our loved ones and stop feeling so tired of working so hard. This change comes from being empowered ourselves. An empowered person gives freely and can keep giving endlessly. At the end of this book in section 14, we share simple ways to empower yourself from within.

In listening for changes, we get excited with the slightest differences, which lets them feel inspired to remember. We reward them by saying, "Oh, I did not know the hat was red," no matter how many times they told us the hat story. We make a conscious decision that from this moment on, absolutely each and every conversation we share with them will be seen as brand new. In doing so, we turn every repeat conversation into an opportunity to help them want to make new neural connections, we spark their brain with positivity, and we invite the dialogue!

When working with ponies, it takes thousands of hours in "Whoa School" to begin to have a slightly safe pony. This means we repeat the exact same thing over a thousand times without losing our patience even once. A good horse trainer rewards the pony every time they hear the word, "Whoa," even when the pony steps on them. Only a positive interaction will empower the pony to try.

I have stood in a pasture thousands of times with a young pony, walking slowly, saying, "Whoa," and stopping. I then excitedly say, "Good," when he gets it right or I say, "Back," and gently back him up when he steps on me. Somehow I have an amazing amount of patience with ponies and have spent endless hours using just three words: whoa, good, and back. I have such patience with a pony and my husband deserved the same dedication, patience and devotion.

If we get mad or rough with a pony, if we say "No," or "Stop," instead of "Whoa," the pony will shut down and stop trying. Everything we want to do with him will become harder for him and for us. We can ruin a pony by failing to see every interaction as brand new and not rewarding him with a loving embrace every single time he is even willing to try and work with us.

With my husband, changing how we approached him after his stroke had to begin with us. The patience I needed with my husband was the same patience I needed in Whoa School, and a million times more important! You must have it in your mind that you will do the same thing a thousand times with kindness and patience and will not lose your cool because their healing depends on it.

Embracing this perspective change that all conversations are new allowed my family to meet every challenge differently. In all of our daily interactions, it was no longer his responsibity to remember. We stopped drawing attention to his memory loss which kept him from feeling bad about it. It was now our responsbility to be present and live in the right here and right now with him. There was no past and no future to any conversation, there was only the here and now.

We made numerous errors by pointing out my husband's mistakes and when we did we clearly noticed him shutting down. We had to increase our efforts to get his heart back into the proccess of healing. Step by step we corrected ourselves, our family and our close friends, as we all began to interact with him as if all conversations were new. Slowly, we taught ourselves to talk to him in affirming and positive ways. Then it began to happen: we no longer saw the loss, we met the time together with a smile and he felt total encouragement to connect with us in everything. He no longer felt he was making mistakes constantly which empowered his healing.

For a long time I wasn't sure if he was really remembering better or if we were just hoping he was. Interestingly, we never put time restraints on any of it. My husband is Hawaiian, so his idea of time is not the same as mine. I want everything organized and planned in advance whereas he prefers not having a set schedule for what will be next. I didn't actively try to do this his way, but I suppose in trying to heal him, we innately approached things more the way he would want to do them. There were no expectations in how fast or slow we went, or how far he would come in this journey.

We wanted to give my husband a real chance to be everything he loved about himself before the stroke. We listened to many repeated conversations that were all new for him and he was excited to talk to us. He was happy to be part of what we were doing.

One day there was no way to deny his memory was profoundly better. He started to surprise me with what he knew on his own, what he recalled from the day before, what he knew from five years ago and then 10 years ago. He knew things about his life that we didn't know and when we checked with others, he was right. It was happening, he was empowered to remember.

We were living, laughing and loving life just as we had before the stroke. He still had some memory glitches as he had no recall of those who were not usually around him. Yet when a new "old" face (someone from his past that he had not seen since his stroke) appeared and smiled as they shared a story, he began to remember them. For those of us always by his side, he was back and he was himself again. Just like Whoa School, there comes a day when you can relax because all the hard work has paid off and whoa means whoa, it's just a fact and you embrace the success.

8
All Memories Have Some Truth

In working with my husband, it was easy to feel frustrated with everything he failed to remember. He mixed up key points, forgot the names of our children, their dates of birth and birth order. He would repeat things or try to enter a conversation and miss the entire point.

One afternoon I was going to the bank when my father informed us that two hens had gotten out of the hen house. My husband asked why we wanted to cook two chickens for dinner.

"No, the chickens are loose," I said.

"Well then let's take them back to the store," he said.

"No, let's put them back in the hen house," I said.

The rest of the day my husband was fixated on going to the store to return the chickens and upset that we went to the bank instead of the store. If had criticized his endless focus on the chickens or the store he would have stopped talking. I finally gave in and made chicken for dinner and he promptly informed me he wanted a hot dog. No matter how circular the conversation was, we needed my husband's brain to be tuned in and excited to keep trying. It was not easy to do, but it was vital to his healing.

One morning, an older son shared a dream he had and I listened intently. The dream made no sense, but I remained focused on the dream and validated my son's feelings about the dream. I realized, that just like my son, my husband needed this same attention and just like dreams, all memories have some truth to the person who experienced it.

My husband needed us to believe in him and listen intently to whatever he had to say just as I had done for my son's dream. He needed us to realize that all memories have some truth and for us to be willing to look for words we could nod to and agree upon. This perspective change took us out of the negative cycle of always pointing out or reminding him what he had wrong or what he had forgotten. We no longer noticed what he was unable to recall.

With this new mindset, we began to search for what was true in everything he did remember. It no longer mattered if he got 99% of the memory wrong, we focused on that 1% success! His brain was now free to catch every wave and to take every risk in organizing the fallen leaves of memories. He could fearlessly drop in to each and every opportunity to interact with us. In using this approach we stopped holding him back from healing. My big wave charger was now back on a board riding the brain waves and feeling totally at ease and embraced. With every word he said we celebrated what was right and he became empowered to talk with us and remember even more.

Chicken or hot dogs, who cares? He wanted to go to the store and not the bank, he had remembered where I was going and where we went. He WAS remembering!

9
Rebuilding New "Old" Memories

The Hawaiian culture honors the power of healers. Part of my husband's recovery came from his 100% native Hawaiian family and not medical intervention. My husband's grandfather and great grandfathers were well-known healers. This belief in healing is part of his lifetime of memories and long before the stroke, my husband believed his nephew also held this power.

I myself met an elderly woman who stated that as a child she was paralyzed after an accident and was unable to walk. She has x-rays from then that confirm she should not be able to walk. She detailed to me personally how my husband's Hawaiian grandfather breathed the *Ha* upon her, in which she stood up able to walk and dance instantly. I also saw my husband heal one of our sons and one of our grandsons, bringing them back to a full healthy life when medical intervention gave them little or no hope.

My husband suffered a bi-thalamic stroke due to a birth defect that had created microscopic holes in his heart. When he first had the stroke, he could not walk, talk, or see. I was so scared because he had always told me that I was never to let him end up in a wheel chair or unable to care for himself. He was a proud man and never wanted anyone else to have to care for him.

My husband and I are very different and we both have a huge sense of pride and a great sense of faith. I was raised as a Christian in the Midwest, and taught that religion is the experience of others, while faith is your own experiences with God. I was raised to explore faith on my own. In searching for God, I have come to believe in the power of prayer, and in miracles.

When my husband had his stroke, I did not want to lose him, but I did not want this strong surfer to end up a shell of his former self and lost to us forever. So I asked God to show me a rose as a sign that my husband would be alright and that I should be determined in helping him regain his life. It was after midnight when a young nurse came into his room and wrote her name on the board over his head. Her name was Rose, and I my heart filled with hope that empowered me to fight for him.

I called his nephew and asked him to visit my husband. When he came into the room we asked my husband if he recognized my voice or knew who I was. He mumbled the wrong name and pulled away from us. Our nephew placed his right hand on my husband's shoulder, my husband turned, looked at our nephew and greeted him. Our nephew asked, "Uncle, who is the woman?" He looked at me and said my name. He could instantly walk, talk and see, but we soon realized he had massive memory loss. He was miles ahead on his recovery physically, but not psychologically.

From all our work in *Mana Gardening*, Dr. Shine and I have come to believe that the mind wants and needs beneficial memories. When faced with tragedy, people heal easier if they tell themselves a better ending. The brain knows the truth, but it prefers the safer story. I began to wonder if we could use some of these concepts to lay down new "old" memories and help my husband reclaim his memories. I reached out to his sister and mother who lived together on another island and asked them to let him come stay for a while so they could share their memories and photographs of his life as child. He went there for almost a week and when he came home he was calmer and happier than he was before he left. He also began to recall on his own some of his childhood memories of his two older brothers, one that had passed away and one that lived on another island.

I had no way to know what his mother and sister shared or which memories were his or theirs. Within a few months, I was certain that on his own, he was remembering more and more about his family life growing up. He wasn't just telling me what they told him, he seemed to be adding to the stories. I am convinced that having these new "old" memories of his life from his mother and sister, is the key to his being able to access some of his own memories.

I began to work on creating more new "old" memories. I built new "old" photo albums and we looked at pictures as I shared with him the stories I knew around them. There were photos from his life before we were married, but I did not have any memories of his older children when they were young. I tried to tell him the sweet stories of their life as adults, however he only remembered that they had been hurtful to him recently and he became angry. I had to be careful in sharing a new "old" memory to ensure I was not connecting him to negative emotions and memories. He needed his older children to share happy new "old" memories of their childhood with him, but they were angry that he could not remember them and did not understand his struggle.

He began remembering organically on his own. Long ago, he shared a story of his oldest daughter as a baby, so I showed him a baby picture and told him that story. He listened and exclaimed how cute and funny she was that day. Then he sat the picture down and said, "That is not her. She was not a chubby baby." I looked at the picture carefully and realized he was right, I had a picture of his youngest daughter, not his oldest.

We began actively working to add new, "old" memories. He remembered a lot about our life together and our youngest children. He remembered many things about their childhood, but he could not recall their birthdates or the times we took them on vacation. I started with stories about their lives as babies and little by little we worked our way to the present time. Each time I shared a story, he recalled more and more about our youngest children and his life with them.

At first, my husband was fragile emotionally. It took very little to make him cry, or become angry. We had to go slowly because he tired easily. We did not tell him what we were doing or why. We did not say he had forgotten or that he needed to talk or that he should listen. We simply chatted with him about the sweet pieces of the past. There were no expectations, just time together, living life.

Everything that was funny or happy brought him into the discussion. Any unhappiness seemed to flip a switch in his entire demeanor. It was if his brain was only accepting beneficial memories. He was not able to process anger in a productive way other than to refuse to talk. His injured brain shut down as a self-protective reflex in the midst of painful or angry emotions or memories.

My husband was also experiencing a delay in his short-term memory storage. Whatever happened today, would disappear from his memory for two to three days. Once three days had passed, he could remember all of it. This only slightly improved. If he was going to need to recall yesterday, we had to create new "old" reminders of the day before, because what we talked about today he could remember. We brought things from yesterday back to today by giving him clues.

If we talked today, he would remember it today. If we talked about yesterday, he was not able to remember that we stopped at Costco, or that he picked me up from work. If today I said, "Oh, you're playing music tomorrow and you have to be there at 1:00." He would not remember this tomorrow. I had to tape signs to the door, put post-it note messages on the mirror and always treat the time between today and three days ago as a potential loss. If I wanted him to remember something from yesterday, I had to make sure he was aware of what is required, today. Or I had to talk about what I wanted him to remember for three days straight. I opened my eyes to understanding his memory pattern and that I had to set him up to NOT fail.

Re-building new "old" memories helped him reclaim his own stored memories and helped him successfully pass through his day-to-day responsibilities without being recognized as memory impaired.

10
Relearning as Learning

Before the stroke, my husband was an accomplished musician who had written many of his own songs. He was skilled in playing guitar, ukulele, harmonica, and piano. He loved to play music, and it was our normal routine for him to practice while I made dinner. We do not have television in our living areas. The TV we have in our bedroom is only for movies. We have a rule with our kids that they can stay up as late as they want if they are playing music, so singing together and enjoying music is our normal family life.

After the stroke my husband struggled to find his voice and had difficulties playing even his favorite guitar. He could not remember any of the music he had written on his own or we had written together. In the evenings he became withdrawn, hiding out in our room until called for dinner. I don't think he realized what had changed but he new something was missing. Our first efforts to get him back into music left him feeling depressed and confused. There was a time when I feared that this part of our lives was lost forever.

It was our youngest twin sons that rescued music for their Dad. They kept singing and soon he was singing along with them. They were young at the time, but my husband had already taught them many traditional Hawaiian songs. These were songs that he had learned as a child – songs he had sung for years with his mother, brothers and sister. The act of singing with the children laid down new memories that aided him in recalling not only his own childhood memories, but memories of playing music with all of his children. Once again, I saw clearly that when we lay down a happy memory that links to the old happy memory, the brain gets busy and works to retrieve the lost data.

One of our sons can pick out the key of anything we sing or play. His twin brother is skilled at holding a rhythm and together they created an easy way for their Dad to relearn the songs he taught them before the stroke. Since one twin knew the rhythm and the other knew the key, they could correct him. I never let the children compare his skills now to how he played in the past. With the boys, my husband replayed the same song over and over like anyone learning a song for the very first time. My husband had to relearn how to do all kinds of things he had already known how to do. We never told him he was relearning anything, just that he was learning.

When it came to songs my husband wrote before the stroke, my sons created new "old" memories of the ones we knew. The children taught him these songs he wrote as if they were new, and did not tell him that it was something he had forgotten. Once he mastered the song, we let him enjoy playing it and then told him, "What a beautiful song you wrote!" We consistently kept our perspective that all experiences are new and kept everything as positive as possible. My husband was relearning as learning, and as the music returned to our home, my husband began to hum and sing joyously.

My husband looked forward to evenings again. And on his own, he started to practice guitar and ukulele whenever we were busy with homework or household chores. The important part here is that he practiced whenever we were focused on other things, and this is something he used to do before the stroke. He returned to doing a familiar routine once he started to recall happy memories that he felt connected to. Where would we be if I had chosen to the standard medical path? He would likely be a medicated zombie simply coexisting with us. It was not enough to deal with him, I wanted to heal him.

Before the stroke my husband was earning a degree in Hawaiian studies. After the stroke, he knew he was getting a degree and he wanted to finish it but he could not remember the courses he had taken, or what he was studying. He could not recall the Hawaiian language but oddly he knew quite a bit of French and he has never been to France. The mind is quite mysterious. However, when we sang in Hawaiian, he understood exactly what the words meant and if we made any mistakes in how we pronounced the words he would correct us right away. The knowledge was there buried away somewhere in his brain.

He kept asking to go back to college. With his short-term memory issues, I was worried we would set him up to fail miserably and he would become depressed. One day, I agreed to enroll him in a class and this was an interesting moment in our lives. He had no idea what degree he was seeking and he made no effort to enroll on his own or look at what he could or even wanted to take, he was just determined to go back to college.

I enrolled him in entry level guitar class and he agreed. Then ukulele, voice, and piano. We did not chat about it at all. He learned as a new student and was never pressured. His love of music returned and he flourished. His music was different in many ways and as he became re-skilled, he began to play songs we had never heard him play before. Most were native Hawaiian songs he had sung in his childhood. He began to recall playing them and surprised us often with something from his past that only he knew. The new "old" memories were linking his brain and bringing forth things we had never heard. He was relearning as learning and with music this process flowed faster than anything else we tried.

Still, he could not remember songs he had written on his own. I could give him a new "old" memory of songs we wrote together, but I had no way to link him to the music he wrote without me and never wrote down or recorded. One day, I found a letter he had writen and made into a song. Our son read the words and remembered the melody. My huband listened to him singing and recalled the song instantly. For now, the rest of the music he wrote remains lost.

In relearning language skills, I made a great mistake. My husband had heard the Hawaiian language his whole life, but he was raised in English. Once he regained his music, I enrolled him in Hawaiian language classes. I thought an entry level class would be as easy as the music. I did not realize that the teachers were not native speakers. They pushed him to break down the sentences as English is taught. He struggled and felt failure. He shut down for a while and became despondent. He barely passed the class which made it even worse because he was then sent on to suffer with level two. The feeling of failure led to worse failures.

When his nephew prayed in Hawaiian, my husband understood what was said easily, and I realized my mistake. I had forced him to learn in a way that was strange to him. There was no connection of happy memories in this process. Because this experience was filled with negative energy and failure, his brain shut down to relearning his language. We now take Hawaiian language as a family in a community-based system with native speakers and he is happy to relearn as learning. It's been slow and I fear that the damage of trying to relearn in a criticizing manner from non-native speakers will take longer to undo. We fully realized that his healing is only possible when criticism and failure are totally removed.

11
Refusing All Negativity

It is hard to face memory loss and not feel stupid. It is hard to live with someone suffering from memory loss and not feel they are just being stupid. You spend a lot of time in a circle, trying to simply move one step. It becomes a reflex to just feel, act, and think that this is all so very stupid. In facing all the day-to-day life challenges, it is easy to forget how fragile the mind and brain really are, especially when the impaired is a tall, strong man. With one negative word or even one inconsiderate action, those suffering with memory loss shut down. To truly help the impaired, you have to get very clear on safeguarding the entire healing process and actively refuse all negativity.

Get clear minded on this as caring for someone struggling with memory loss is much harder than it seems. You will have to extract and remove from your life every person who makes your life harder. You won't have time to debate or diffuse the situation when someone refuses to adhere to your zero tolerance for negativity. Your health and wellbeing as a caregiver is at stake, and just as importantly, the healing of the impaired depends on it. The impaired can become locked up in their mind if you don't adhere to this principal. The self-absorbed, the demanding, and the needy have to look somewhere else for help for the time being. Your lives are too delicate to risk and they will be for a long time.

12
Offering Concise, Achievable Solutions

In our book, *Mana Gardening, Empower Yourself and Live & Better Life,* we teach a method called the No-Spin Power tool. It requires you to recognize when your mind is spinning out over something, and try to reduce the problem to one sentence that accurately states the true problem. The next step is finding an achievable solution that can fit into one short sentence. This skill is vital to working with those suffering from memory loss.

"We need to talk," or long-winded problem solving sessions were impossible for my husband. We had to become skilled at reducing our problems and finding concise, achievable solutions. Do not expect those with cognitive impairment or injuries to be able to problem solve, debate, troubleshoot, argue, resolve differences, apologize, negotiate or make you feel better. They are not able to handle any of our emotional needs. You cannot say, "You hurt my feelings," and expect to be met with apologies or resolution. Do not waste their valuable healing energy on emotional issues. Consider their healing energy to be absolutely precious. Instead of bogging their minds down with our emotional needs and problems, look for the most achievable solution for each and give them that win, every time.

The No-Spin Power tool has three parts: 1) reduce the problem to one sentence; 2) find an easy, achievable solution; and 3), choose to live happily with or without the solution. This last part set my husband free. He was surrounded by happy people no matter what the outcome, however in reducing the solution to something he could achieve easily, we had many moments when he was our hero!

13
Safely Taking & Making Space

When my husband first came home from the hospital after the stroke, he was often angry and frustrated when he could not remember things. There were some hard times when an extremely negative switch in his brain flipped and his anger was actually scary.

Soon after the stroke his sister called about problems with one of his daughters and he became deeply depressed. I asked his doctor what she thought. She suggested that we try medicating him. She mentioned that we could give him antidepressants and/or perhaps something for anger. I felt sad. On antidepressants, his emotions would be under control. He would never be upset or angry but we would also never really know how he really felt about anything. If we medicated him, how could we ever have the real him fully come back to us? Worst of all, the medications she would prescribe him had side effects of increased memory loss. If we were to put him on these drugs his memory loss would get increasingly worse and he would never be healed.

One day his anger escalated and for a moment, I felt uncertain we were safe. I called my mom to take the kids and I took him to see his doctor. I explained to her my fears. I was afraid to medicate him and I was afraid not to medicate him. She listened to me about wanting to help him heal. She agreed that for now we could try not medicating him, but only if I agreed to call the police if I felt he was placing anyone, even himself, at risk. She also warned me that if I did have to call the police, she would have no choice but to medicate him. There was no room for mistakes. If for any reason his anger escalated, the healing that I had wanted for him might never be possible. I had to navigate very carefully.

I started watching him more attentively and in doing so I saw some patterns. He was quicker to get angry if he was hungry and he was hungry often. He craved ice cream, but since he was slim, calories were not something I worried about. He wanted food all the time, especially between meals. I let go of what he ate, how often he ate and how many sweets he had. I chose to shop more carefully and take us all out to eat at the health food store whenever he agreed. I did not push him to eat healthy. I did not complain about having to cook more or do more dishes. I chose not to notice his eating. I now believe that the healing brain wants more food and craves more sugar because it needs a lot more energy.

I also noticed that his anger escalated whenever I questioned his thought process. He became paranoid about being confused or disoriented. I began to see when his mind was skipping around and he was not able to connect his thoughts. If I pointed out that he wasn't making sense, he became angry. Whenever I noticed he was escalating into anger mode, I had to not engage in any conversations about anything that mattered and especially whatever he was upset about. I let him have his way and if food, or acceptance did not calm him down, I simply gathered up everyone in the car and we went for a drive or to see a movie.

When he was able to calm down, he went with us for the break. When he could not calm down, we went without him, but the key was to simply tell him we would be back soon. In taking space from him I was careful to not add to his anxiety or anger. I had to speak calmly, say nothing about the anger and tell him we will be back soon. I could not argue with him or do anything to mislead him into thinking that we were abandoning him in any way. I had to learn to let him have the last word so he felt in control.

It came down to some basic rules. We could disagree, but we could not get into arguments. We stopped looking for resolutions to problems and we stopped trying to talk when we had problems. At this point, there wasn't space for problem solving (maybe in the future but not now). Whenever any of us felt upset or angry, it was ok to be angry as long as we all took space away from each other. We had to safely take and make space whenever we needed it. We had to learn how to not push back or add negative commentary to a disagreement. We all had to let go of a lot of hurt and disappointment each and every day. We focused on his healing.

There were times when I too felt sad, lonely and even afraid. He spun out badly several times. I marked them on the calendar and tried to track what it would require to avoid the triggers that put him in a negative spin. On the calendar, I could see the angry moments were occurring farther and farther apart. I also learned more about what worked for him and what did not help him at all.

We sought help from a counselor, but at first this was more for me than for him. I felt alone and all of our normal day to day life problems were now mine to handle. We found a counselor who was half Polynesian and half white so she understood both of us independently and as a couple. She gave us many ideas on how to re-connect but most of all she reminded me that I mattered too. She began to work with us on additional ways to help him strengthen his ability to remember. I found having a counselor made the process less lonely as we had someone else to connect with on interpersonal matters and that helped us both feel more connected to one another. We could talk about our lives subjectively and in time, we both saw clearly that we needed to make some space for ourselves and for just the two of us which helped us re-connect emotionally.

14
On-The-Go Meditation
is for Everyone

In our book, *Mana Gardening, Empower Yourself & Live a Better Life* we share important skills based on simple, ancient Hawaiian personal empowerment techniques. In this guidebook we share a tool from that book to help you attain and retain the energy and clarity needed to care for someone with a cognitive disorder.

First is to create your own inner garden in your imagination. Close your eyes and imagine the most beautiful place you have ever been or seen, perhaps some place you have seen pictures of or dreamed about. Now picture that place in your mind and look around there. What do you see? Is there an ocean? Are their mountains? Maybe you see a forest or a luxurious home. Now put yourself in that image and see yourself there. Breathe in and exhale slowly, expelling the air from deep within your lungs.

See yourself in that beautiful paradise, that heavenly place in your mind. Relax there and feel yourself there. Notice if there is there a breeze. Is it warm or cool? Do you smell flowers or food? Feel your body totally relax and bask there for a few seconds. Now open your eyes. You just spent a few seconds relaxing from within and in doing so your body was able to lower its cortisol levels which go with stress and increase your endorphins which can make you feel euphoric. Welcome to your inner garden.

You just created an inner garden in your imagination with your eyes closed and in doing so you felt peaceful, relaxed and at ease. Now I want to take you deeper into what we call *Mana Gardening* practice.

Close your eyes for a few seconds and let me show you how I visualize my inner garden. There is a beautiful crystal clear lake with snow capped mountains far in the distance on the other side of the lake. There are rolling woods and wildflowers on both sides of my lake with trails all along the water's edge. This lake is fed by a waterfall far off in the distance and to one side, the lake spills over and creates a stream that flows gently. By the edge of the lake, there is a stone patio with steps down to the water's edge. It is a warm, sunny day with a cool breeze. In your hands there is a big, soft pool lounge floatie with a built-in drink holder and headrest pillow. You also have a cool drink, you have on comfy swimwear and a nice wide-brimmed hat.

Now open your eyes and hold onto your visualization of my inner garden. See yourself walk down those steps and wade out into the water. You place the floatie down and the drink goes into the little cup holder built into the armrest of the floatie. You climb on, lay back and relax. You're present in your own life and you're also in my inner garden. You're floating along and you can come here whenever life is beyond your control. You are welcome to come here to relax when those around you are negative or stressed, or spinning out.

Let's test it. You stay on that floatie, sipping a cool drink, the water is calm, you can feel the breeze, and smell the fresh air. There on my lake is only you and there is nothing to interrupt your peace. See yourself there floating, relaxed and content. Now, simply relax a few seconds and float...

Can you see yourself still floating there relaxed and happy as you continue to read this guidebook? Congratulations, with your eyes open, you have just practiced On-The-Go Meditation. Simply try to see yourself there in your own paradise or in my inner garden. You do not need time, silence or solitude. This is what makes *Mana Gardening* unique – you can relax, and experience peace and bliss no matter where you are and no matter what is happening around you. Your eyes are closed for a few seconds or can be wide open as you go about your busy day.

You are welcome on my lake anytime. I may be there resting on a big, white, overstuffed chair with a soft foot stool. You can wave to me if you want and I will always smile and wave back. We are sharing the *Mana*, we are being refilled with peace and the energy to face our real lives with positivity. In being a caregiver, you need to release stress as often as you can and dropping into the garden or taking a few minutes to relax in my garden lake can help you decompress from stress. It can also help you rejuvenate and gather energy as needed.

This is vital for you and for those suffering with cognitive impairments. You can re-charge yourself and you can encourage them to picture heaven, to imagine Hawaii, or to pretend they are on vacation. You can both take a few seconds of peace anytime you want or need. We encourage you to try this several times a day. You can share your ideas of paradise with those you care for and you can ask them to describe theirs. It is a simple way to feel better, let go of some stress, and get your mind engaged in positivity. Encourage everyone who is part of this healing process to try this simple system to feel better. It is empowering and builds healthy forthright energy within you. It will give you powerful and life strengthening *Mana* to carry you through as you travel the long road ahead.

For several years my family focused on helping my husband reclaim his memories. Today he is totally self-sufficient and capable of doing everything he enjoys doing. With the help of the local university in arranging tutors and providing extra testing time, he completed his degree. In everyday conversations, he is smart, witty and funny. He is back to playing music and surfing.

He can remember about 90% of what we do today and about 60% of the past. He has a lapse between short- and long-term memory, in which it takes him about three days to recall the days before. He has moments of normal age-related forgetfulness for the phone or car keys, but I have it too, and I have no history of cognitive impairment.

He recalls more old memories as time goes by, however it still requires a new "old" memory to access. When an old friend from high school came to visit us this year, he brought pictures and talked all about their time in grade and high school. After this visit my husband was able to recall decades of detailed memories.

A few months ago, I found some old pictures of our favorite beach, and instantly my husband recalled taking our twin sons there that same day. I went through all the images, one by one, seeing images of the ocean and sea turtles. He kept talking about how little the boys were and then as I flipped to the last image, there was this picture of him with our twins and my heart jumped with joy. He was right! He was empowered to remember!

Keti Kamalani lives on the island of Oahu with her husband and family. She and Michelle Shine, Ph.D. continue to study the use of empowerment-focused approaches to cognitive health and healing. The Mana Gardening Institute, LLC, is a woman-owned, Hawaii-based organization established to facilitate research in forthright personal empowerment. Please drop us a note and share your experiences as you use this book. We would love to know what works for you and those you care for. Visit the website to learn more about Mana Psychology or any of our publications. Follow us on Facebook/Twitter/Instagram under ManaGardening.

www.managardening.com

www.ingramcontent.com/pod-product-compliance
Lightning Source LLC
Chambersburg PA
CBHW040241240726
48664CB00001B/226